100 HAIKU
for the
80s
Generation

Haiku by

KERRIE FLANAGAN

DEAN K MILLER

Layout design by

CARMEN RUYLE HARDY

Hot
Chocolate
Press

DEDICATION

THIS BOOK IS DEDICATED

TO THOSE WHO

"CAME OF AGE" IN THE 80s,

THOSE WHO REFUSE

TO LEAVE THE 80s BEHIND,

AND THOSE WHO

NEVER WANT TO FORGET

WHAT AN AWESOME DECADE IT WAS.

Introduction

The 80s; a bright, neon filled decade that ventured into the new frontier of technology and video games; introduced Madonna, the Bangles and Devo into the music scene; everyone wanted their MTV; Marty McFly was sent back to the future; and fashion definitely made a bold statement. It was a time before cell phones, social media and snap chat.

We wrote *100 Haiku for the 80s Generation* as a way to celebrate this totally awesome era. Each Haiku, made up of only 17 syllables, gives a quick snapshot of iconic moments, places, people, music, television, film and fashion from the 80s. Written to evoke a specific memory, remind you of a forgotten movie or song, a now-dreaded hairstyle, or then fashion statement now turned faux pas, we hope it makes you smile.

We had a blast putting these together and we hope you have as much fun reading them as we did writing them.

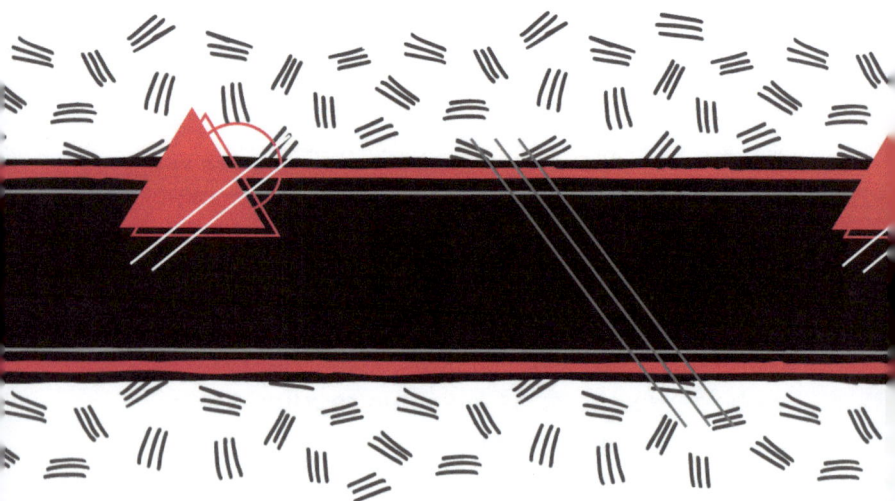

Table of Contents

Chomp dots, run from ghosts
Blinky, Inky, Pinky, Clyde
I want the bonus

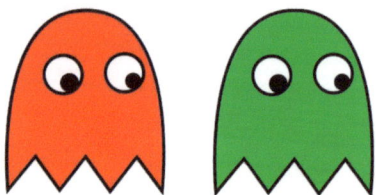

Live vj's hosted
Videos played day and night
It is now extinct

Like, totally dude
That is grody to the max
Gag me with a spoon

Different color squares
Twist and turn to match colors
Way too hard to do

Cujo-Christine-It
Firestarter-Talisman
Did you ever sleep?

Homecoming football
Bonfires, date the quarterback
Taste my Lip Smackers

Ugly little dolls
With a birth certificate
Sheer insanity

Two simple joysticks
New video game system
Atari's the best!

Drinking Wine coolers
Bartles and Jaymes were the best
So many flavors

The old lady asked:
"Where's the beef?" Um, duh, just look
In between the buns!

Crazy looking Koosh
Not really a ball at all
Fun to toss around

In flavors galore
Hubba Bubba bubble gum
Popped sticky on face

80s Culture

Badly drawn pictures
Partners try to guess your clues
Is this an All-Play?

Getting fit in tights
Richard Simmons leads the way
Sweatin' to oldies

Fastest yet to date
Thirty-two bit microchip
Compaq 3-8-6

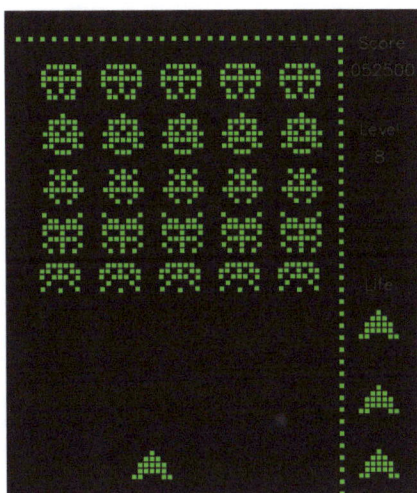

Coke tried something new
Fans rallied for classic Coke
They soon got their wish

In shiny dark suit
And Ray-Ban Wayfarer shades
Pixeled Max Headroom

NBA debut
Michael Jordan is the man
Rookie of the year

Ode To Andrew McCarthy

Pretty in Pink, sigh
Weekend at Bernie's, funny
St. Elmo's Fire, deep

Oh, what a feeling
Sweatshirt hanging off shoulder
Dancing 'round the room

Legwarmers; headbands
Flashdance was a fashion craze
Care to dance again?

Stretch tights, leg warmers
Getting soaked on a dance stage
All about Flash Dance

Aliens invade
Fear not to be abducted
By ET or ALF

Better Off Dead

John Cusack classic
Johnny wants his 2 dollars
Blaine loves girl named Beth

Beth loves someone else
Exchange student speaks English
Well honk my hooters

Must ski K2
Something gets in your way, turn
Monique wins Blaine's love

Ghosts in the attic
Slime trails across the hallway
Who you gonna call?

Kevin Bacon starred
All dancing was forbidden
Footloose by the end

Ex-hippie parents
Cement their family ties
Alex, Mal, and Jen

Detention for five
Brain, jock, convict, spaz, princess
Breaking through labels

The five bratty kids
Never got bagels or juice
In the breakfast club

If you were Kevin
Would you wonder of the years
If you were Winnie?

80s TV & Movies

Blue jeans, hats, and boots
You're such an urban cowboy
Riding the fake bull

New York lady cops
Busted all the city goons
Cagney and Lacey

Working 9 to 5
Secretaries seek revenge
Did they kill their boss?

There's chores to be done
So says Mr. Miyagi
Let's wax on and off

Parents are away
Dance through house in underwear
Start risky business

Hey Marty McFly
Take that gray DeLorean
Back to the future

80s TV & Movies

Maverick flies high
Heading to the danger zone
Wants to be the best

The empire strikes back
Han Solo caught and frozen
Luke leaves swamp early

Ferris says he's sick
Not true; adventure begins
Bueller (pause) Bueller

Chasing the Nazis
Get ark of the covenant
He said, "I hate snakes!"

Treasure map and coin
Got "The Goonies" hunting gold
Of One-Eyed Willie

Sport coat and cool shades
Don Johnson solved city crimes
Miami Vice stud

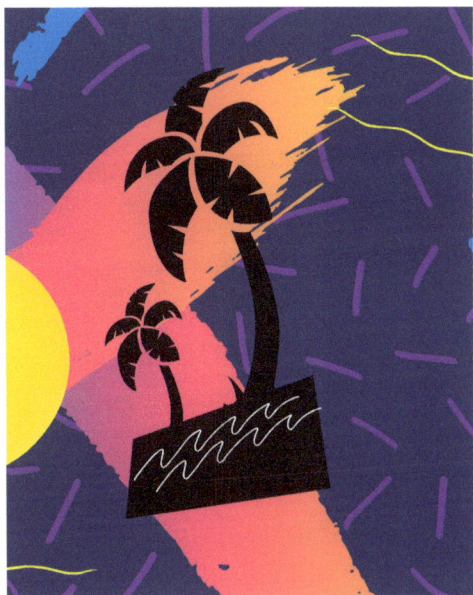

Spock and Kirk on quest
They must travel back in time
To get help from whales

New coach, sketchy guy
Small town kids win tournament
Hoosiers basketball

Forty years of life—
Celie dreams of her sister
The Color Purple

Robot short circuits
He seems to be more human
Wants to stay this way

80s TV & Movies

Little girl finds friend
He is not from planet earth
Helps E.T. phone home

Crocodile Dundee
Responds to the street gangster
"No, this is a knife"

Special forces gang
These heroes couldn't be beat
The A-Team was rad

Corn farmer hears voice
If you build it they will come
Turns out to be right

Athletes versus geeks
Jocks lose the final battle
Revenge of the Nerds

Griswold vacation
Traveling to Wally World
Misfortunes abound

80s TV & Movies

80s MUSIC

Disco faded out
As hair bands rocked concert halls
With power ballads

80s Music

Hair bands were the bomb
Concerts in glitter and flames
Rockin' all night long

She sang "We Belong"
And "Love is a Battlefield"
Pat Benetar rocked

It's close to midnight
The Zombie dance is starting
It's such a Thriller!

80s Music

Did you ever want
To crack that whip while wearing
Flower pots for hats?

Portable music
The cassette slides into place
Love my new walkman

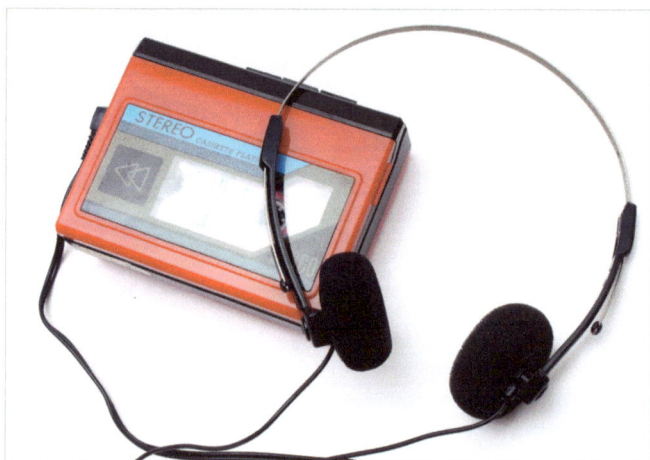

80s Music

I'm all Out of Love
Totally Eclipse of the heart
Mend my broken heart

Artist from up north
Cory Hart sang in his shades
Sunglasses at Night

My future's so bright
Even on a cloudy day
I gotta wear shades

80s Music

When Steve Perry led
Journey was top on the charts
Don't Stop Believin'

Boy George, I didn't
Really want to hurt you then
So please stop asking

If you have to say
"Do That To Me One More Time"
Find another friend

I think I love her
In that second hand store hat
Raspberry Beret

Weird construction job
Using only rock and roll
We built this city

Portland band Nu Shooz
Scored their first big hit record
"I Can't Wait" was it

80s
Music

Michael Jackson move
Debuted on Motown Special
Glides across the floor

Sand between your toes?
Let's walk like an Egyptian
So sang the Bangles

80s Music

An all female band
Insisting We Got The Beat
So get on your feet

Leave the boys at home
'Cuz girls just want to have fun
And who can blame them

What fun can you be
Adam Ant? Don't drink, don't smoke
You goody two shoes

Ninety-nine balloons
Anti-war protest in red
What color were yours?

80s Music

Singing with long beards
ZZ Top struts and tops charts
"Sharp Dressed Man" and "Legs"

Fighting world hunger
Music stars align as one
Sing "We are the world"

Hey there Phil Collins
My new cassette player skips
Sus, Sus, Sudio!

80s Music

Bon Jovi, White Snake
Hair envied by all the girls
Screaming guitars ruled

Curling iron hot
Curl, curl, curl, hairspray to hold
How big was your hair?

Horse riders wore first
Stirrup Pants became the rage
With leg warmers, too

Without a zipper
We managed to wear button
Fly five-oh-one jeans

80s Fashion

Polka dots and stripes
Electric neon colors
Loud and bold, totally rad

A decade of big
Hair, shoulder pads and sweaters
Bright, bold jewelry

Let's get physical
Aerobics was all the craze
Leg warmers a must

80s Fashion

Make your skin glisten
I like it when you're sweaty
Let's get physical

I like the dress but
What's the deal with shoulder pads?
Your purse that heavy?

Alligator shirts
Collar turned up, lookin' cool
Why not wear two?

Big and puffy boots
Not meant for walking on moon
A fashion statement

80s Fashion

A jean mini skirt
Big slouchy socks and white keds
Polka dotted shirt

Saved money for a
Brightly colored plastic watch
Had to have a Swatch

Fold jeans over first
Then carefully roll them up
Now you are ready

80s Fashion

Ponytail holders
Colors, sizes, fabrics, more
Scrunchies hold your hair

Lace, fingerless gloves
Madonna leading the way
Frilly mini-skirt

80s
HISTORICAL
EVENTS

Sleeping mountain wakes
Mount St. Helens blows her top
Then slumbers again

Need to fill the tank?
Eighty-nine cents per gallon
Was the cost of gas

Fairy tale wedding
Televised for all to see
Charles and Diana

Watching on T.V.
The space shuttle Challenger
Explodes after launch

Seven million join
Hands Across America
Fighting poverty

Former movie star
Gets the role of a lifetime
Ron is President

Joint expedition
Finds the shipwreck Titanic
History unsunk

Big hair and bright clothes
The 80s generation
Totally awesome!

KERRIE FLANAGAN

As a teenager in the 80s, Kerrie embraced everything that made this decade totally awesome. Mornings were spent curling her hair to achieve the perfect feathered style. She and a friend frequented the local convenient store to stay sharp on Centipede, PacMan and Galaga. At the age of 13, Kerrie attended her first concert at McNichols Arena in Denver (which is sadly no longer there) to see Journey. She became an instant fan and soon, obsessed with the group. She listened to their music constantly, read magazine articles about them, watched MTV with the hopes of seeing one of their videos and she even joined the Journey fan club. Her room became the Journey shrine (a term coined by her mother). Every bit of wall space was covered with posters, signs and anything related to the group.

Besides being a Journey fan, she also loved being in band. She played clarinet, piano, saxophone and even a few years of cello. High School added marching band to her life. She loved the competitions, the traveling, the excitement and especially the friendships. Following high school graduation, she became an elementary school teacher, a wife and a mom. Now, life is taking her in a new direction as a writer, publisher, and writing consultant. Her kids are grown and she and her husband are enjoying this next phase in their lives. But, she will always have fond memories of the great music, MTV, quirky movies, bright fashions, video games and everything that made the 80s the best decade ever.

www.KerrieFlanagan.com
www.HotChocolatePress.com

DEAN K MILLER

Though Dean began writing short stories and poetry in the early 80s, much of his time was spent keeping his hair curly and permed, attending to his Kenny Loggins'-style cropped beard, and a brief stint in dance classes, leg-warmers included.

Always one to root for the underdog, any 80s music playlist Dean loads will be filled with one-hit wonder songs: Whip-it, Turning Japanese, Wondering Where the Lions Are, 99 Red Balloons, Beds Are Burning, and more. The decade ended with a wedding (almost 30 years and counting,) a growing family and new adventures.

Now there's not enough hair to perm, the beard comes in grey, but the music playlist favorites haven't changed. Miller spends his days as a training staff specialist for the Federal Aviation Administration, fly fishing, and writing. Learn more about his published work at www.deankmiller.com

CARMEN RUYLE HARDY

Carmen enjoyed many benefits of growing up in a small, rural town in Colorado. Life and time moved a little more slowly there, so the 80s hung around well into the 90s. Luckily her family stood by her and her blue eye shadow, and Walkmans were allowed on her 45-minute schoolbus ride. Long live Bon Jovi! Carmen tight-rolled her jeans and came of age in a junior high hallway filled with Aquanet. Early-morning curling iron efforts could not be lost midday!

Her aunt and her aunt's mother owned the hometown newspaper and gave Carmen her first writing and graphic design gigs when she was in high school. They sat her down at a 9-inch display and showed her how to use a mouse. Carmen was in awe of the endless possibilities of the Classic Mac – which most likely had a 4 MB limit! When her aunt let her help take the pasted-up ads and floppy disks with text to the neighboring town, Carmen watched lines of letters roll out of the typesetting machine and fell head over heels for the printed word.

Later on at Colorado State University, that same Aquanet aerosol would come in handy as a fixative for charcoal drawings. Since then, her good luck and hard work have resulted in finding inspiration by traveling near & far, brainstorming art and volunteer possibilities, jumping on board with intriguing freelance projects and seeing the world through the eyes of her two children.

www.bycarmencita.com

More books from Hot Chocolate Press

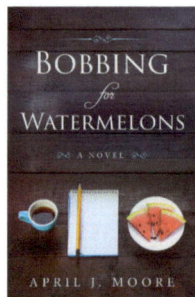

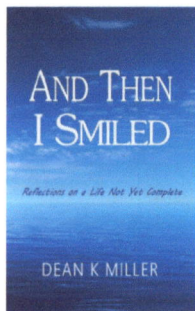

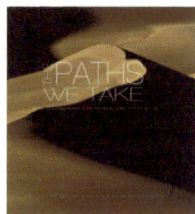

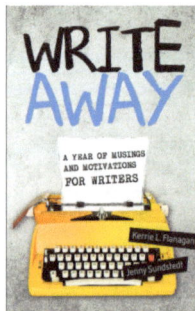

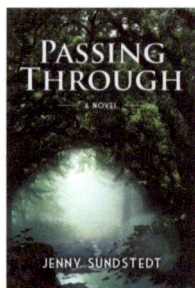

Echoes
Reflections Through Poetry and Verse
Dean K Miller

BOBBING for WATERMELONS
A NOVEL
APRIL J. MOORE

AND THEN I SMILED
Reflections on a Life Not Yet Complete
DEAN K MILLER

THE PATHS WE TAKE

WRITE AWAY
A YEAR OF MUSINGS AND MOTIVATIONS FOR WRITERS
Kerrie L. Flanagan
Jenny Sundstedt

PASSING THROUGH
A NOVEL
JENNY SUNDSTEDT

All books
are available
on
Amazon.com

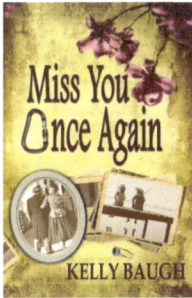

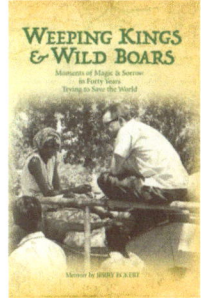

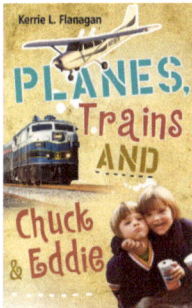

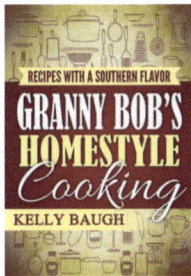

Miss You Once Again

KELLY BAUGH

BEAUTY
SURROUNDS US

Claire's Christmas Catastrophe

By
Kerrie
Flanagan

WEEPING KINGS
& WILD BOARS

Moments of Magic & Sorrow
in Forty Years
Trying to Save the World

Memoir by JERRY ECKERT

Kerrie L. Flanagan

**PLANES,
Trains AND
Chuck & Eddie**

**Claire's
Unbearable
Campout**

By
Kerrie
Flanagan

RECIPES WITH A SOUTHERN FLAVOR

**GRANNY BOB'S
HOMESTYLE
Cooking**

KELLY BAUGH